Machines with Power!

Airplanes

by Derek Zobel

BELLWETHER MEDIA
MINNEAPOLIS, MN

Blastoff! Beginners are developed by literacy experts and educators to meet the needs of early readers. These engaging informational texts support young children as they begin reading about their world. Through simple language and high frequency words paired with crisp, colorful photos, Blastoff! Beginners launch young readers into the universe of independent reading.

Blastoff! Universe ★

BLASTOFF! DISCOVERY

Grade 4

BLASTOFF! READERS

Grades 1-3

BLASTOFF! Beginners

Reading Level · Grade K

Sight Words in This Book 🔍

a	in	people	this	you
are	is	see	time	
do	it	sit	to	
has	look	the	up	
have	on	them	water	

This edition first published in 2021 by Bellwether Media, Inc.

No part of this publication may be reproduced in whole or in part without written permission of the publisher. For information regarding permission, write to Bellwether Media, Inc., Attention: Permissions Department, 6012 Blue Circle Drive, Minnetonka, MN 55343.

Library of Congress Cataloging-in-Publication Data

LC record for Airplanes available at https://lccn.loc.gov/2020007089

Editor: Amy McDonald   Designer: Andrea Schneider

Printed in the United States of America, North Mankato, MN.

Table of Contents

What Are Airplanes?

Look up!
Do you see
an airplane?

Airplanes
are machines.
They fly in the sky.

Parts of an Airplane

Wings lift airplanes. **Engines** give them power.

wing

engine

9

Airplanes have
a **cockpit**.
Pilots sit in it.

cockpit

This airplane
has wheels.
It lands on
the ground.

wheels

This airplane
has **floats**.
It lands on water.
Splash!

floats

Airplanes at Work

This is a fighter jet. It patrols the sky!

This is a
cargo plane.
It carries goods.

cargo

People ride
in this plane.
Time to fly!

Airplane Facts

Airplane Parts

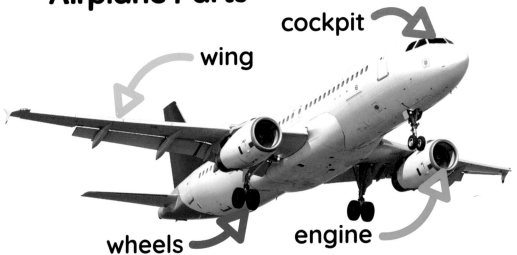

cockpit

wing

wheels

engine

Airplane Jobs

patrol
skies

carry
goods

move
people

Glossary

cargo

goods moved by vehicles or airplanes

cockpit

the part of an airplane where a pilot sits

engines

parts of airplanes that make them go

floats

parts that help some airplanes land on water

To Learn More

ON THE WEB

FACTSURFER

Factsurfer.com gives you a safe, fun way to find more information.

1. Go to www.factsurfer.com.

2. Enter "airplanes" into the search box and click 🔍.

3. Select your book cover to see a list of related content.

Index